Schaum Making Music Piano Library

Theory Workbook

Level Two

By Wesley Schaum

Schaum's Pathway to Musicianship

The *Schaum Making Music Piano Library* integrates method, theory, technic and note reading with appealing materials for recital and repertoire. Schaum's well-proven motivational philosophy and sound pedagogy are widely recognized.

PREFACE

This workbook presents basic music theory intended to supplement any Level Two method book and for all ages. Melodic and harmonic interval reading are emphasized because of their importance for note reading and for training the sense of touch. The student should become accustomed to the feeling between the fingers to form the space needed to play each interval. The scale fundamentals presented here lay the groundwork for more analytical study of scales later. Scale fingerings for both hands are shown separately on the back inside cover.

The pages should be checked and corrected before the "keyboard assignment" is started. **Regular keyboard practice of these workbook pages is essential** to reinforce the learning process. A brief music dictionary is presented on the back inside cover.

INDEX OF LESSONS

ISBN 978-1-936098-14-9

Exclusively Distributed By

Visit Hal Leonard Online at
www.halleonard.com

World headquarters, contact:
Hal Leonard
7777 West Bluemound Road
Milwaukee, WI 53213
Email: info@halleonard.com

In Europe, contact:
Hal Leonard Europe Limited
42 Wigmore Street
Marylebone, London, W1U 2RY
Email: info@halleonardeurope.com

In Australia, contact:
Hal Leonard Australia Pty. Ltd.
4 Lentara Court
Cheltenham, Victoria, 3192 Australia
Email: info@halleonard.com.au

Lesson 1: Inner Leger Lines

Name____Date_________________Score_________________

LEGER LINES are short extra lines used to extend the staff up or down. Middle C is the most common note written on a leger line.

Leger lines *below* the *treble* staff may be thought of as "borrowed" from the top of the bass staff. Leger lines *above* the *bass* staff are likewise "borrowed" from the bottom of the treble staff. This is illustrated in the line of notes below.

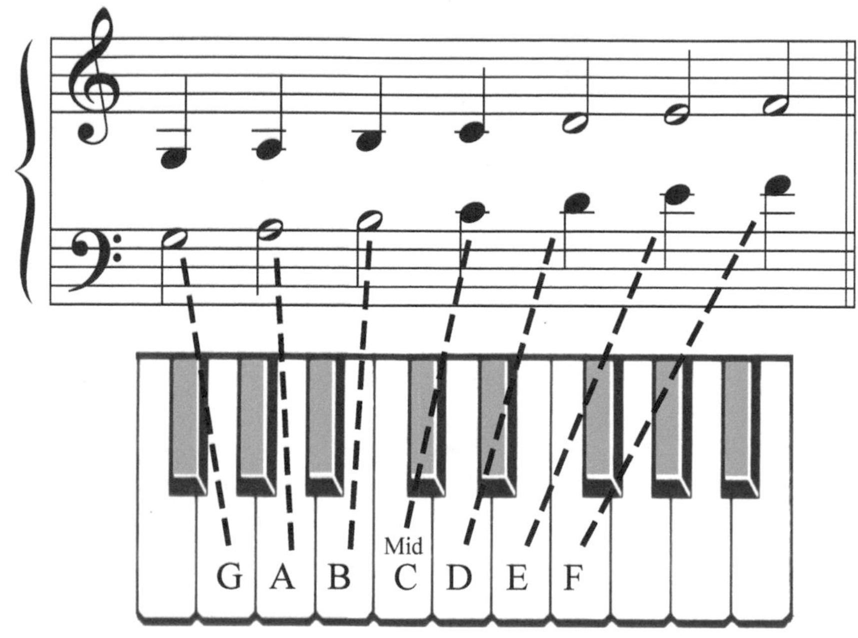

Notes with *stems up* are for Right Hand.

Notes with *stems down* are for Left Hand.

DIRECTIONS: Write the letter names in the box below each note.

KEYBOARD ASSIGNMENT: After completing the written work, play all notes at the keyboard at least three times per day. Say the letter names aloud as you play.

Lesson 2: Inner Leger Lines with Accidentals

Name________________________________Date________________Score________________

DIRECTIONS: Write the letter name in the box under each note. Include a sharp or flat as required by each accidental.

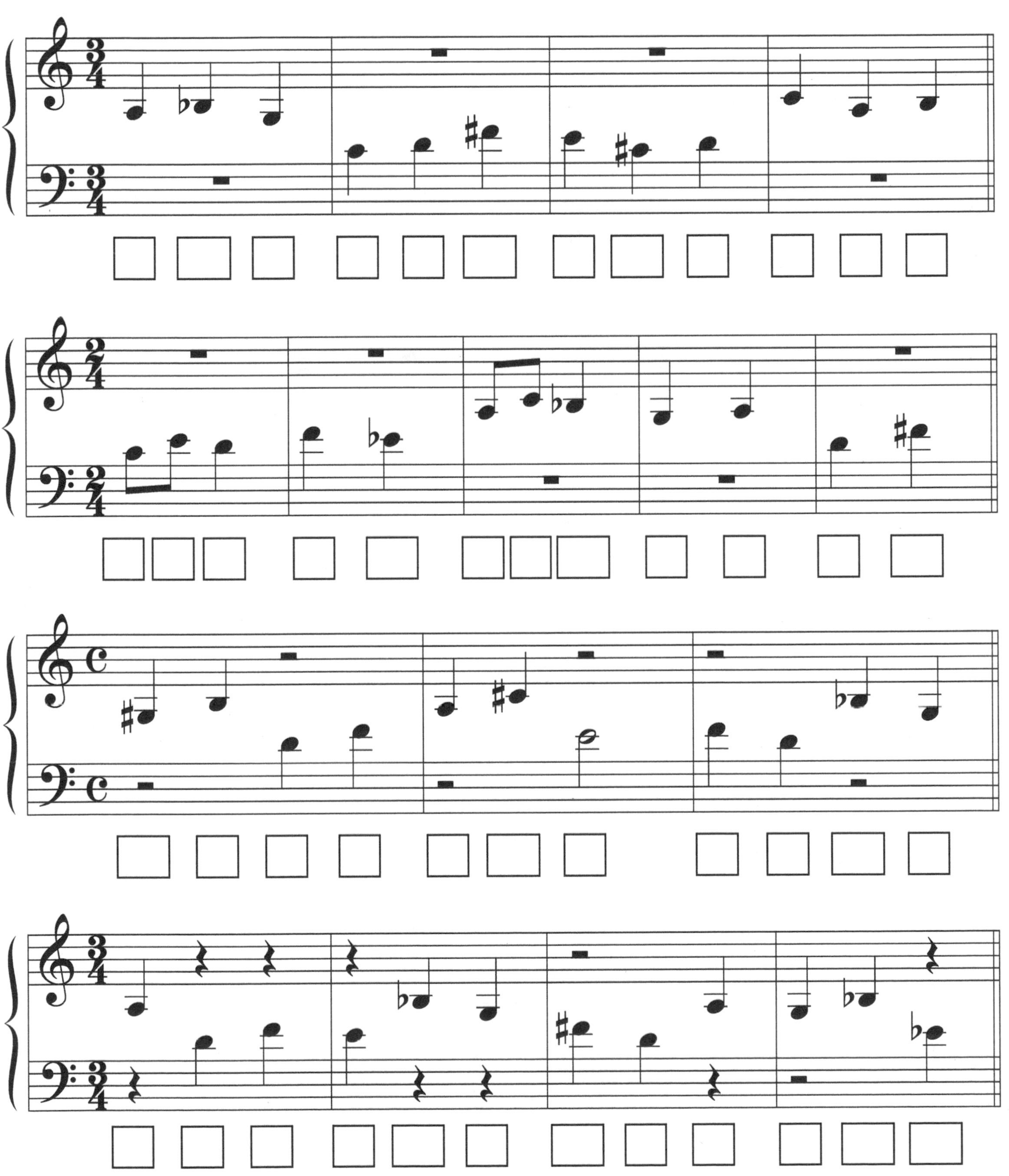

KEYBOARD ASSIGNMENT: After completing the written work, play all notes at the keyboard at least three times per day. Say the letter names aloud as you play.

Lesson 3: Harmonic Interval Reading

Name____Date__________________Score__________________

An interval is the distance between one note and another. The interval number is the same as the number of alphabet letters, as shown on the line below.

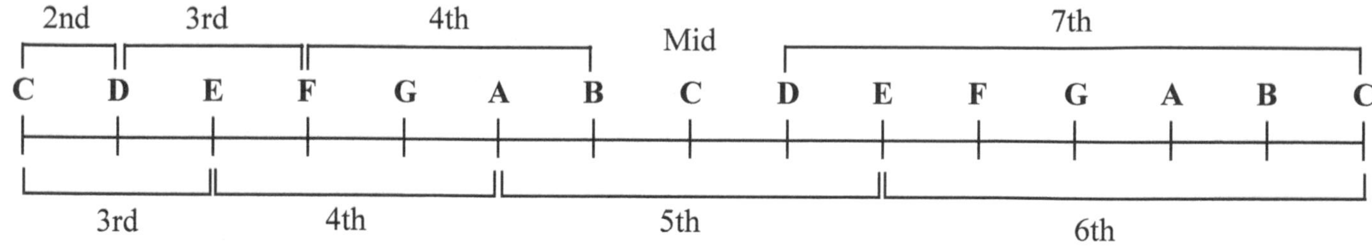

DIRECTIONS: Write the letter names in the stack of boxes *below* each interval. Count the number of letters on the alphabet line. Write the interval number in the wide box *above* each interval.

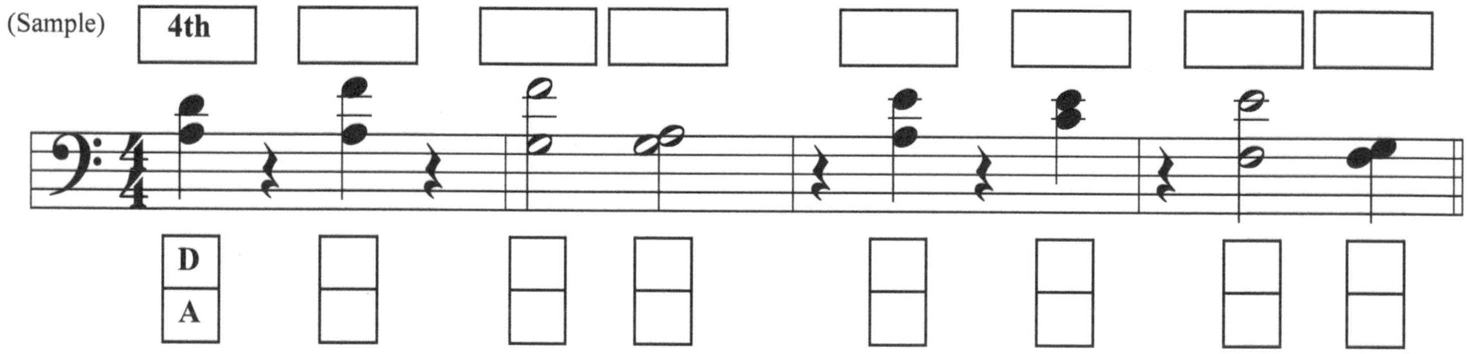

(Sample) **4th**

D
A

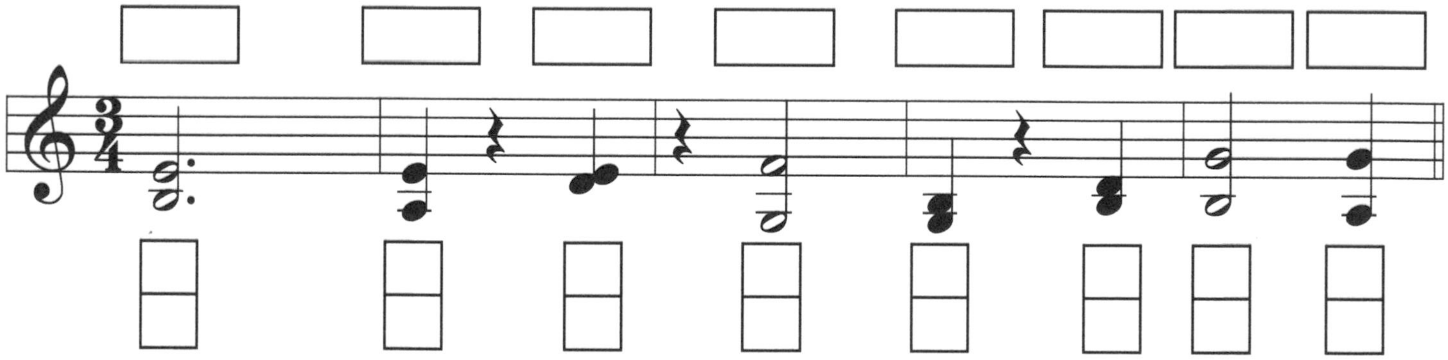

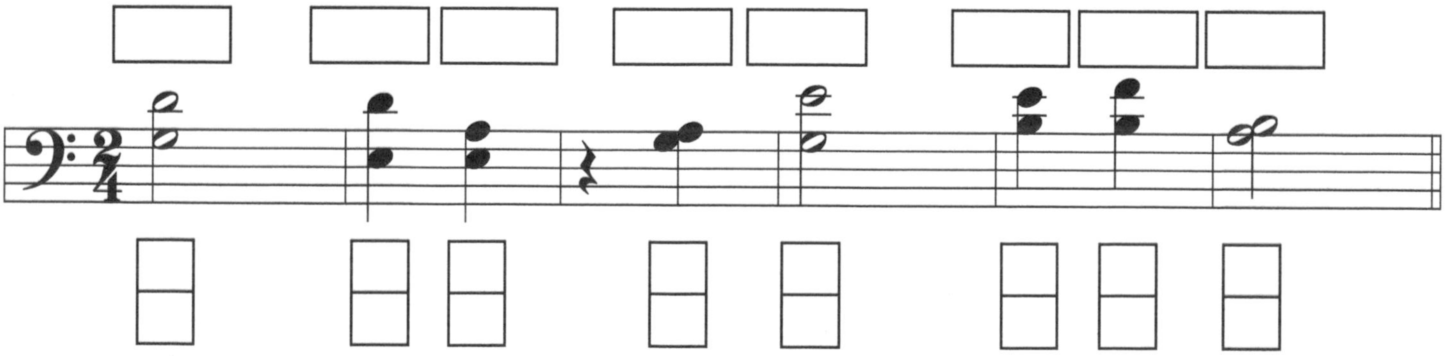

KEYBOARD ASSIGNMENT: After completing the written work, play the notes in each measure. Say the interval number aloud as you play. Do this three times per day.

TEACHER'S NOTE: Interval playing is an opportunity to develop the *sense of touch.* The student should be aware of the *feeling in the hand,* while forming the space between fingers needed to play each interval.

Lesson 4: Interval Reading with Key Signatures

Name____ Date__________________ Score__________________

DIRECTIONS: Write the letter names in the stack of boxes *below* each interval. Include a sharp or flat when required by the key signature. Write the interval number in the wide box *above* each interval. Sharps and flats *never* affect the interval number. If necessary, count the number of letters on the alphabet line on the preceding page.

KEYBOARD ASSIGNMENT: After completing the written work, play the notes in each measure. Say the interval number aloud as you play. Do this at least three times per day.

TEACHER'S NOTE: It is assumed that the proper fingering of intervals has been gained from technic study in Schaum's *Fingerpower®, Level 1*. If not, it should be assigned at this time.

Lesson 5: Major Scale Construction: A Major

Name____ Date____________________ Score____________________

The MAJOR SCALE is a pattern of *whole steps* and *half steps* in musical alphabet order. The eight notes of the major scale have number names called *degrees*. The keyboard shows the *C Major Scale* with degree numbers printed below each letter. The two *Half Steps* are indicated by a slur and the letter H. All other steps are *Whole Steps*.

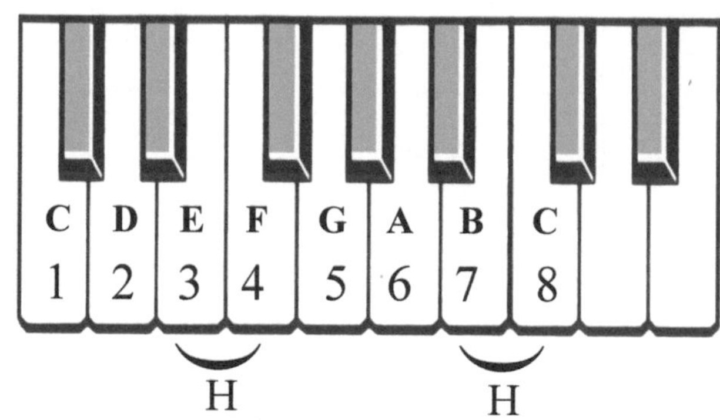

Notes of the *A Major Scale* are shown below with scale degree numbers. The letter H shows the location of the two *Half Steps*.

DIRECTIONS: Add sharps where necessary to make the pattern of *Whole Steps* and *Half Steps* for the *A Major Scale* in both staffs. Write letter names, including the correct sharp, in the box below each note.

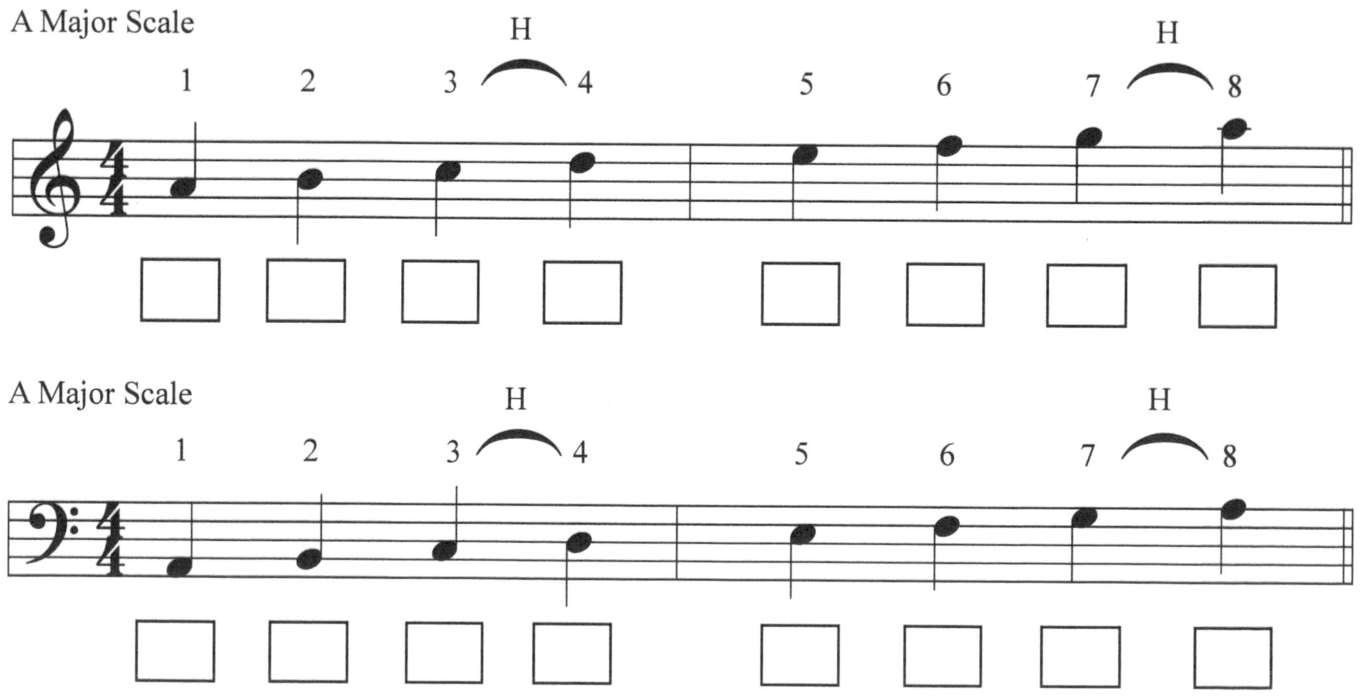

KEYBOARD ASSIGNMENT: After completing the written work, play the A Major Scale with each hand, using the fingering shown on the **back inside cover**. Do this at least three times each day.

TEACHER'S NOTE: It is recommended that the student be *at the keyboard* when doing the written work on this page.

Lesson 6: E-flat Major Scale and Key Signature Review

Name____Date___________________Score__________________

Notes of the *E-flat Major Scale* are shown below with scale degree numbers. The letter H shows the location of the two *Half Steps*.

DIRECTIONS: Add flats where necessary to make the pattern of *Whole Steps* and *Half Steps* for the *E-flat Major Scale* in both staffs. Write letter names, including the correct flat, in the box below each note.

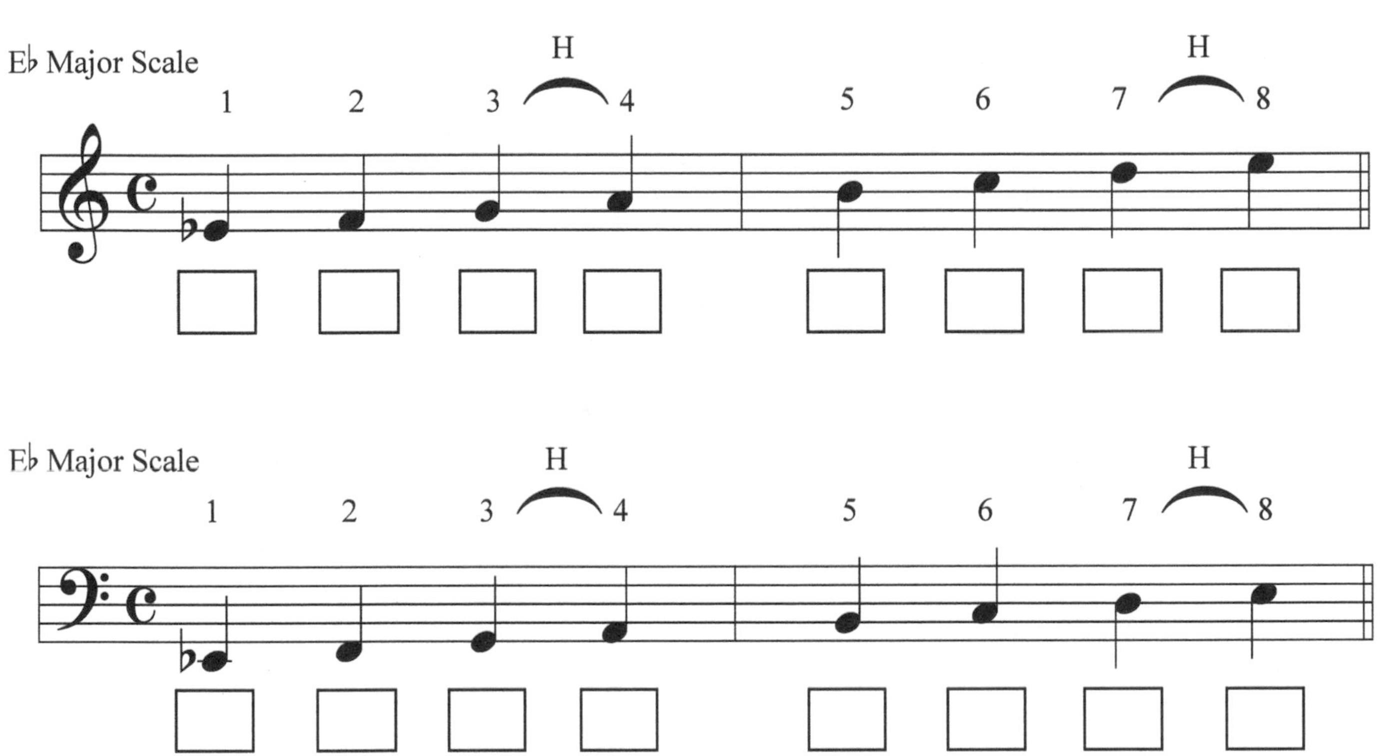

DIRECTIONS: Write the letter name of the key on the line below each measure. If necessary, refer to the **back inside cover**.

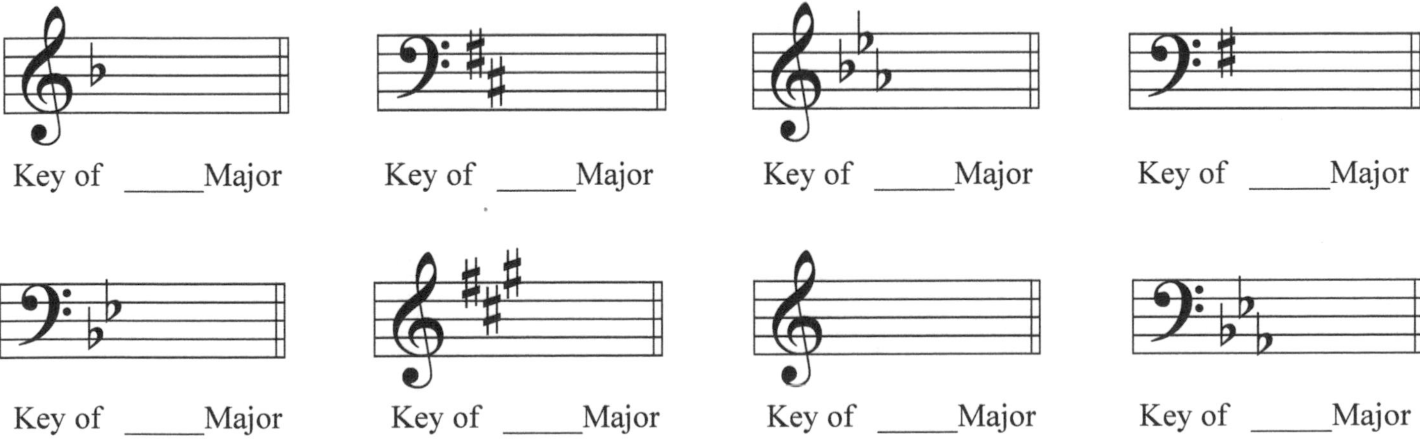

KEYBOARD ASSIGNMENT: After completing the written work, play the E-flat Major Scale with each hand, using the fingering shown on the **back inside cover**. Do this at least three times each day.

Lesson 7: Upbeat (or "Pickup") Notes

Name____ Date____________________ Score____________________

*An UPBEAT (or "Pickup") occurs when the *first note* of a piece is NOT the first *count* of a measure. An upbeat may consist of several notes and can occur with *any* time signature, as shown in the sample lines below.

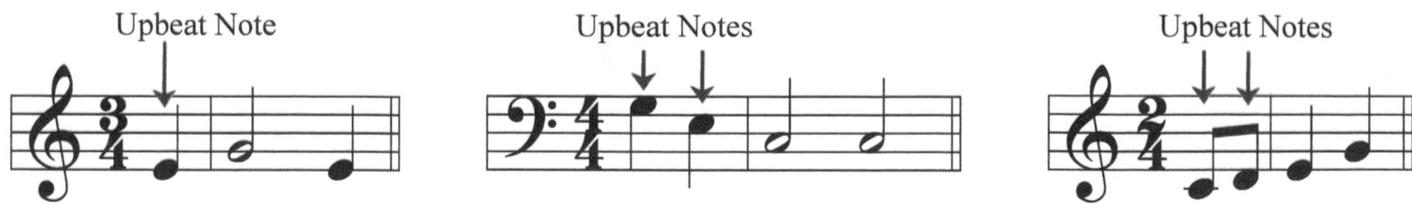

DIRECTIONS: Draw a circle around the *upbeat* notes in each line of music below. Then, write the counting on the dotted lines for every measure, as shown in the sample. Watch for *different* time signatures.

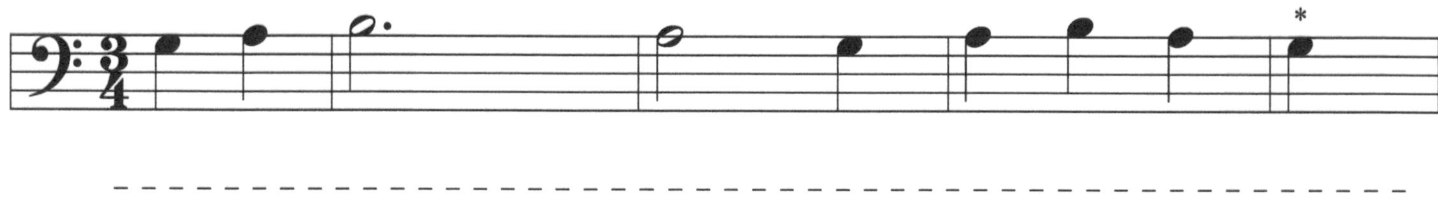

KEYBOARD ASSIGNMENT: After completing the written work, play each line of music. Count aloud while playing. Do this at least three times per day.

*The counts missing at the beginning of a piece are usually (but not always) borrowed from the final measure of a piece. This depends upon the individual composer or arranger. Together, the upbeat counts at the beginning and the counts left over at the end make one complete measure.

Lesson 8: Damper Pedal Marks

Name_______________________________ Date______________ Score______________

The DAMPER PEDAL is farthest to the *right* in the group of 2 or 3 pedals of a piano. Its purpose is to blend sounds together and help create a legato effect. It is played with the toe of the *right* foot. The heel should always be *kept on the floor* when using the pedal. The most common pedal mark is shown below.

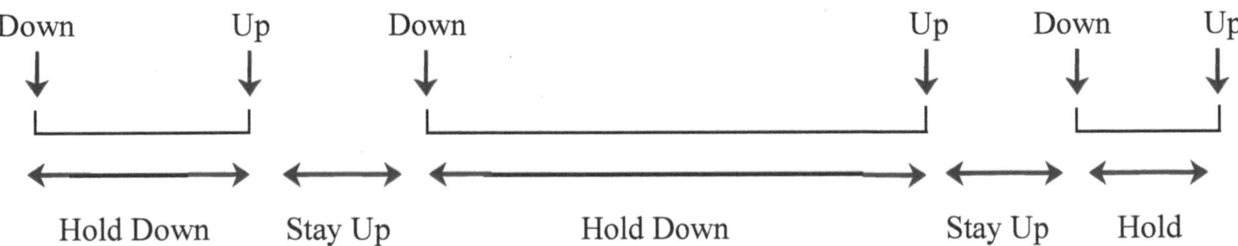

Another type of pedal mark is often called the *syncopated pedal* or *legato pedal*. It is used to avoid blurring one note or chord into another. The pedal is raised at the same time as the hands play the keys, but the pedal is lowered immediately afterward. This is shown in the following illustration.

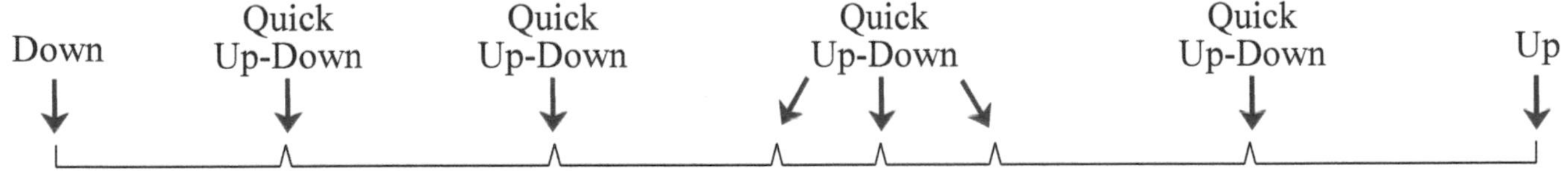

KEYBOARD ASSIGNMENT: Play the lines of music above using the damper pedal as marked. Do this at least three times per day. Play very slowly at first, then increase the tempo a little with each day's practice.

TEACHER'S NOTE: Use of the damper pedal varies widely among different composers, performers and editors. Therefore, specific pedal marks may differ from one edition to another.

Lesson 9: 6/8 Time Signature and Counting

Name______________________________ Date______________ Score______________

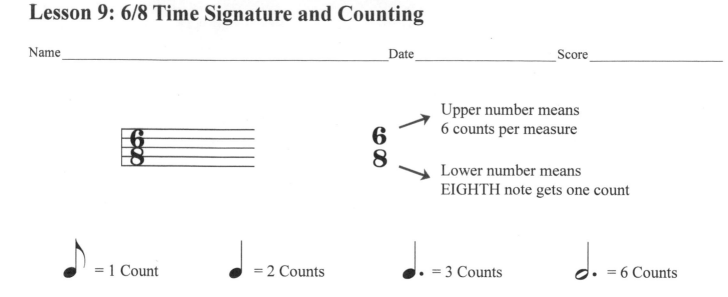

6/8

6 → Upper number means 6 counts per measure

8 → Lower number means EIGHTH note gets one count

Eighth note = 1 Count

Quarter note = 2 Counts

Dotted quarter note = 3 Counts

Dotted half note = 6 Counts

DIRECTIONS: Write the counting numbers on the dotted line below each measure (see samples). Be sure the numbers are spaced evenly in each measure.

RHYTHM ASSIGNMENT: After completing the written work, count aloud and clap hands, one clap for each note. Do this at least three times per day. For extra work, the same measures may also be played at the keyboard while counting aloud.

Lesson 10: Rests in 6/8 Time

Name ______________________________ Date ______________ Score ______________

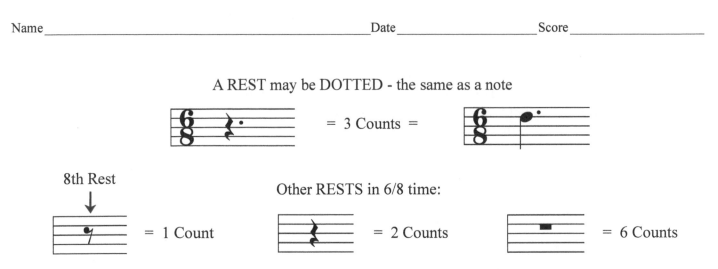

A REST may be DOTTED - the same as a note

= 3 Counts =

8th Rest

= 1 Count

Other RESTS in 6/8 time:

= 2 Counts

= 6 Counts

DIRECTIONS: Write the counting numbers on the dotted line in each measure (see sample). Be sure the numbers are spaced evenly in each measure. Watch for *pickup* notes.

KEYBOARD ASSIGNMENT: After completing the written work, count aloud and play each line of music. Do this at least three times per day.

Lesson 11: Chromatic Scales

Name______________________________________Date__________________Score__________________

The CHROMATIC SCALE is a series of notes that proceed by *half steps*. A chromatic scale may begin on any black or white key; there are 12 notes in the complete scale. Although there is no special way to "spell" a chromatic scale, *sharps* are usually used for *upward* movement; *flats* are usually used for *downward* movement. The two lines below show the chromatic scale beginning on A, moving up and down.

Finger numbers have been printed above every note. Notice that the 3rd finger always plays every black key in right hand and left hand, both upward and downward.

DIRECTIONS: Add accidentals (sharps or flats) as needed to form *chromatic* scales in each line below. Do NOT add any accidental to the *first note* of each line.

KEYBOARD ASSIGNMENT: After completing the written work, play the chromatic scales using the correct fingering, as shown in each line. Do this at least three times per day. For extra work, play a long chromatic scale using all keys of the keyboard, up and down.

TEACHER'S NOTE: The ending note of each chromatic scale is not printed here to allow more room for the student to write the necessary accidentals.

Lesson 12: Accent Marks

Name____Date____________________Score____________________

A note with an ACCENT mark is played with extra stress or emphasis – somewhat louder than notes without accents. These are the three common accent marks:

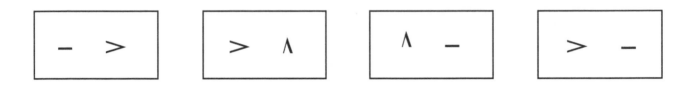

– = small accent > = medium accent ∧ = big accent

DIRECTIONS: Compare the accents in each box below. Draw a circle around the *softest* one in each box.

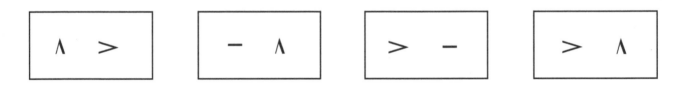

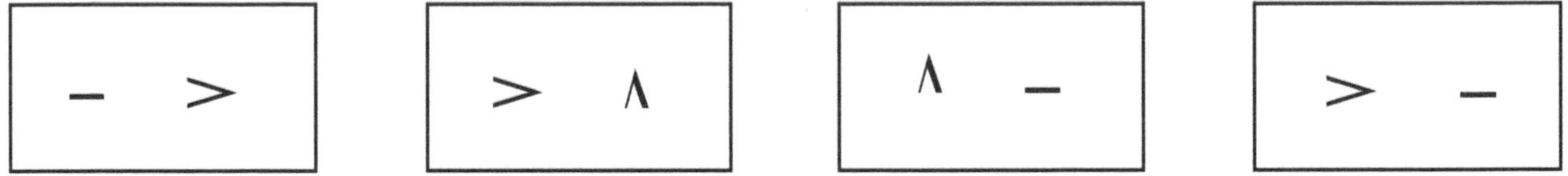

DIRECTIONS: Compare the accents in each box below. Draw a circle around the *loudest* one in each box.

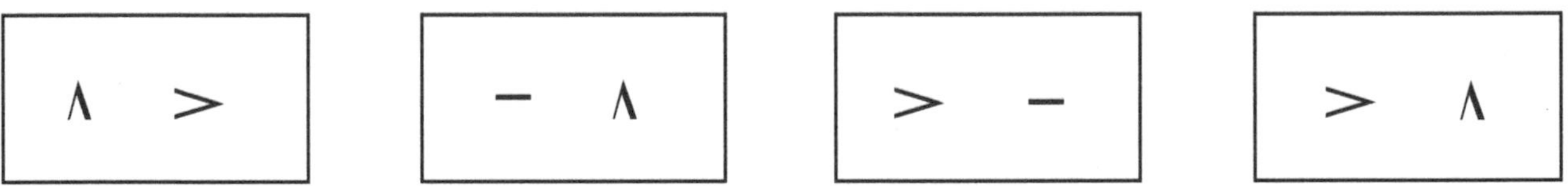

DIRECTIONS: Circle the accents in the lines of music below. In the 2nd line, notice how accents show where the melody moves from one hand to another.

KEYBOARD ASSIGNMENT: After completing the written work, play both lines of music. Be sure to play each kind of accent differently. Do this at least three times per day.

Lesson 13: Outer Leger Lines

Name______________________________ Date______________ Score______________

This illustration shows various notes below the bass staff and above the treble staff.

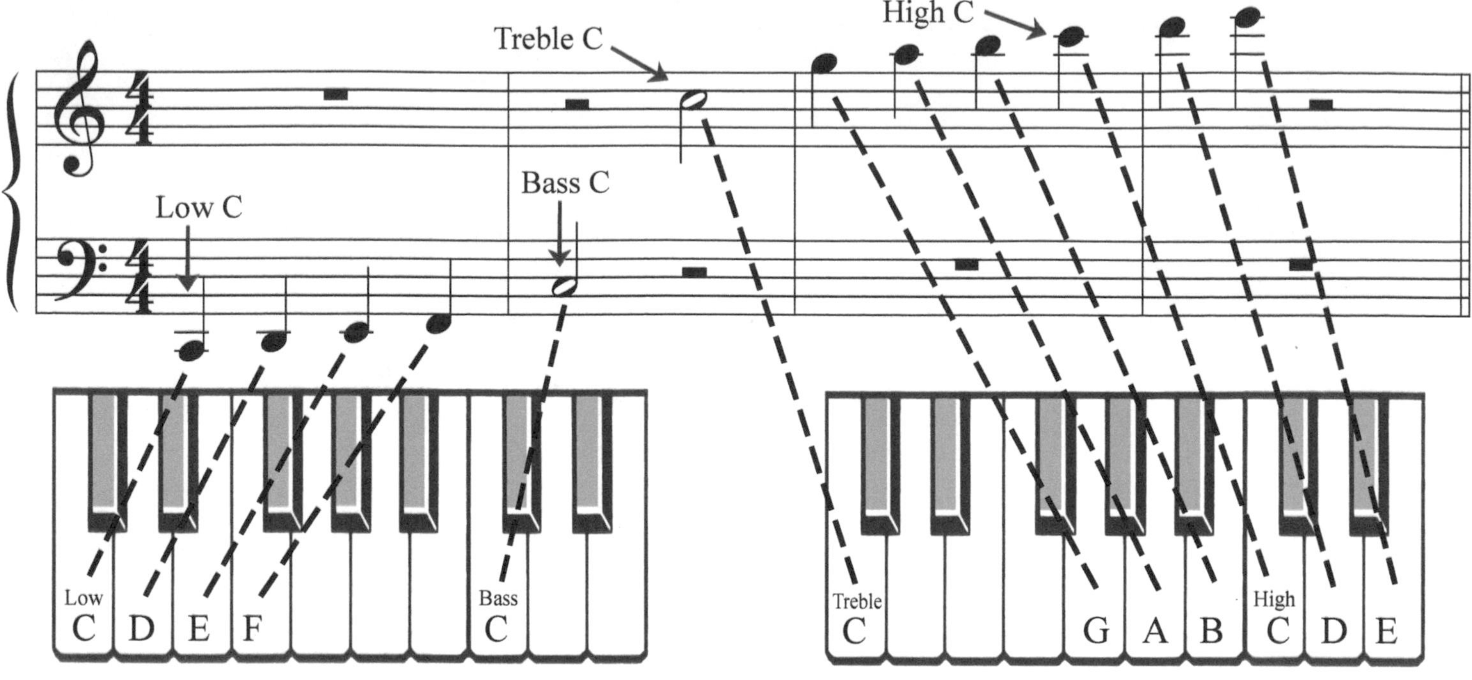

DIRECTIONS: Write the letter name in the box below each note.

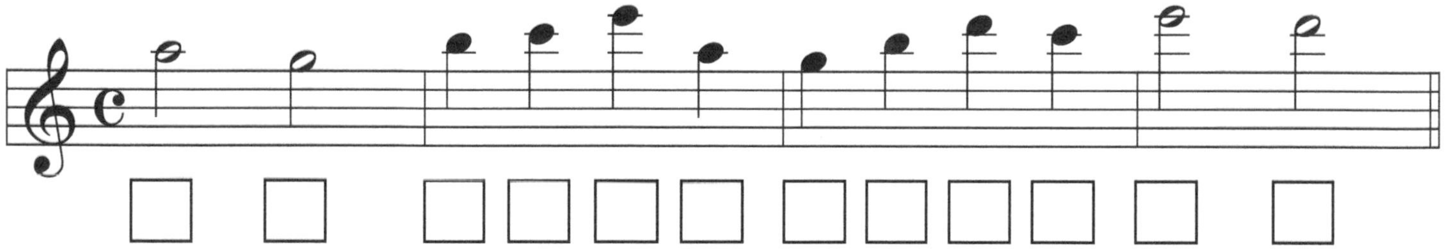

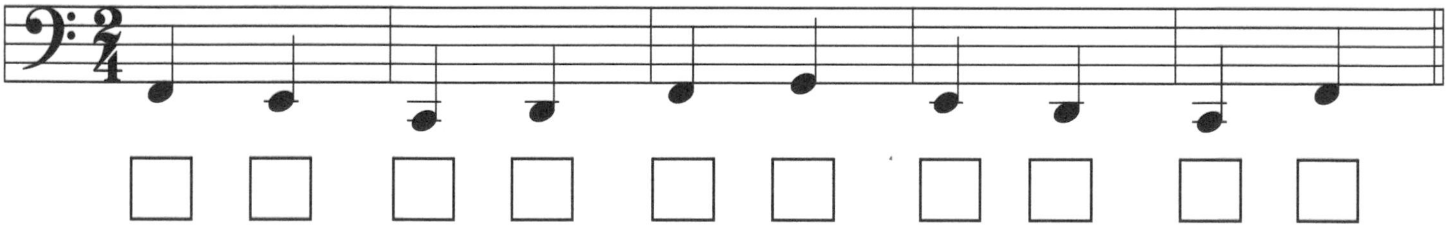

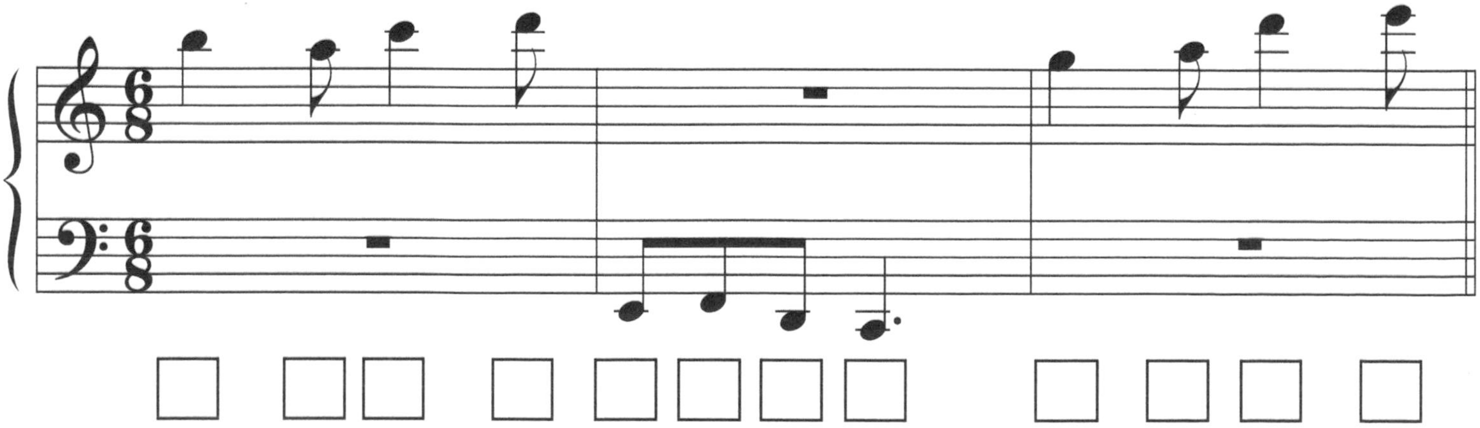

KEYBOARD ASSIGNMENT: After completing the written work, play all notes at the keyboard three times per day. Say the letter names aloud as you play.

Lesson 14: Musical Terms

Name____ Date__________________ Score__________________

Italian words are usually used to give directions describing the tempo, loudness and mood of music. The Italian pronunciation of these words is used in speaking English.

DIRECTIONS: Look at the dictionary on the **back inside cover**. Write the definition of each word on the blank lines below. Practice pronouncing each word as shown.

accelerando ...(ahk-sell-er-ON-doh) means ______________________________

agitato ....(ahd-jih-TAH-toh) means ______________________________

alla marcia ....(ah-lah MAHR-chee-ah) means ______________________________

a tempo ....(ah TEHM-poh) means ______________________________

cantabile ....(cahn-TAH-bil-lay) means ______________________________

crescendo ......(cre-SHEN-doh) means ______________________________

diminuendo ....(di-min-you-END-oh) means ______________________________

dolce ....(DOL-chay) means ______________________________

leggiero ....(led-jee-AIR-oh) means ______________________________

lento ....(LEN-toh) means ______________________________

marcato ....(mahr-CAH-toh) means ______________________________

presto ....(PRESS-toh) means ______________________________

spiritoso ....(spir-ih-TOH-soh) means ______________________________

vivo ....(VEE-voh) means ______________________________

Some Italian terms like *con, molto* and *poco a poco* are always used with other words to form different meanings; therefore you will have to look in two different places in a dictionary to find the complete definition.

DIRECTIONS: Look at the dictionary on the **back inside cover**. Write the definition of each set of words on the blank lines below. Practice pronouncing these words as shown.

con anima ....(kone AH-nee-mah) means ________________________

con brio ....(kone BREE-oh) means ________________________

con moto ....(kone MOH-toh) means ________________________

con vivo ....(kone VEE-voh) means ________________________

molto allegro ....(MOHL-toh ah-LEG-grow) means ________________________

poco a poco accelerando (POH-koh ah POH-koh ...) means ________________________

Lesson 15: Repeated Notes in Adjoining Intervals

Name______________________________ Date________________ Score________________

Interval reading is made easier when you compare intervals next to each other to see if any notes are the same. Such notes are called *repeated notes*.

Repeated notes may be at the top or bottom of the intervals. Sometimes the repeated note is at the top of one interval and the bottom of the next interval. Repeated notes are shown by dotted lines in the following samples.

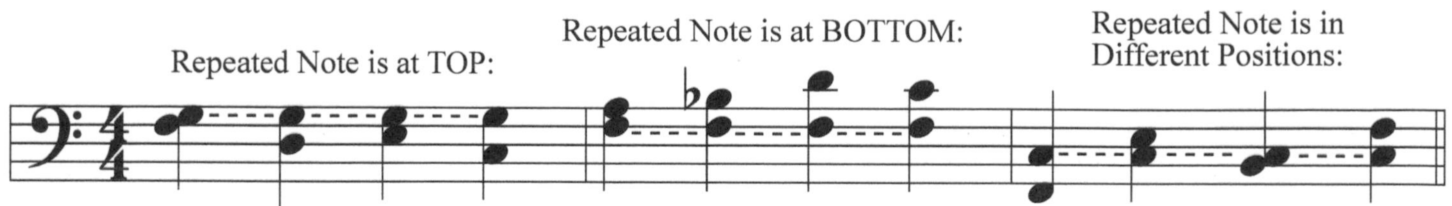

DIRECTIONS: Compare the intervals below, looking for *repeated notes*. Write the letter names of the repeated notes in the appropriate box. (Boxes should be left blank if the note is *not* repeated.)

Draw dotted lines connecting the repeated notes; draw a dotted line connecting the letter names of repeated notes in the boxes, as shown in the samples.

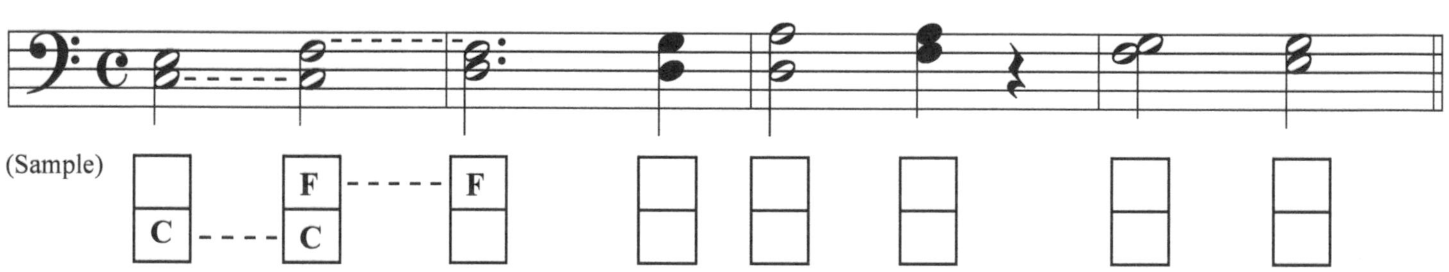

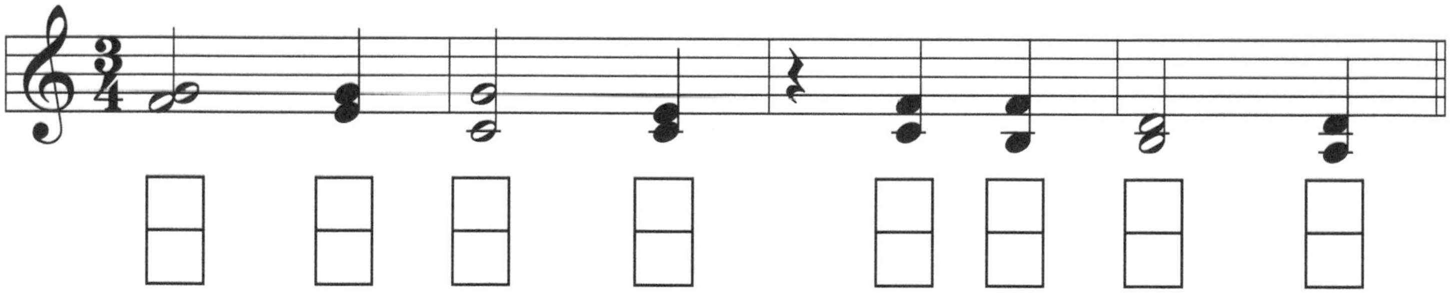

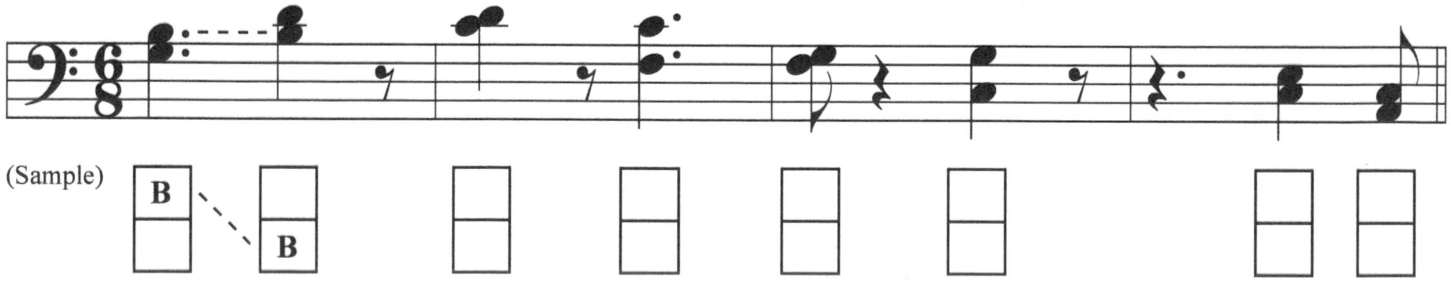

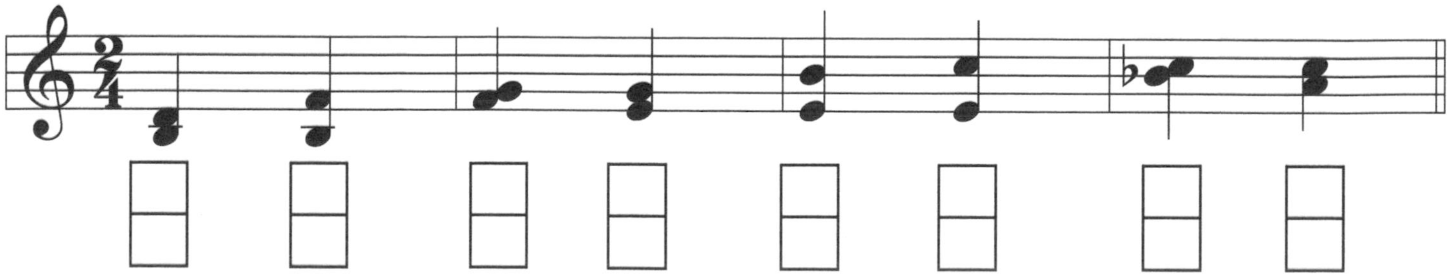

(Sample) C - - - C; F - - - F

(Sample) B - - - B

KEYBOARD ASSIGNMENT: After completing the written work, play the intervals in each measure. Do this at least three times per day. For extra work, add letter names in the *blank* boxes.

Lesson 16: Repeated Notes in Adjoining Chords

Name____Date____________________Score____________________

Repeated notes also make chord reading easier. The repeated notes may be the top, middle or bottom note of adjoining chords as shown by the dotted lines. Sometimes there may be *two* repeated notes, as shown in the sample line below.

DIRECTIONS: Compare the chords below, looking for *repeated notes*. Write the letter names of the repeated notes in the appropriate boxes. (Boxes should be left *blank* if the note is *not* repeated.)

Draw dotted lines connecting the repeated notes; draw a dotted line connecting the letter names of repeated notes in the boxes, as shown in the samples.

(Samples)

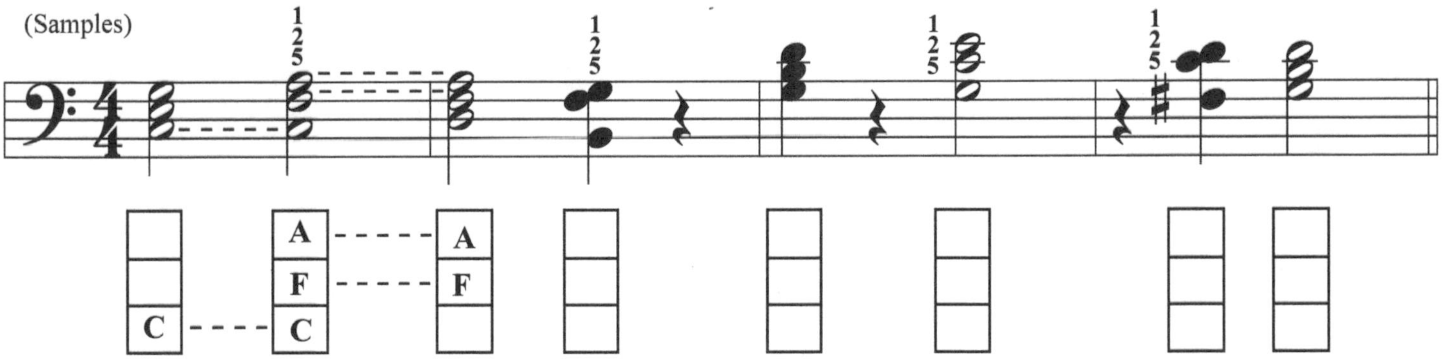

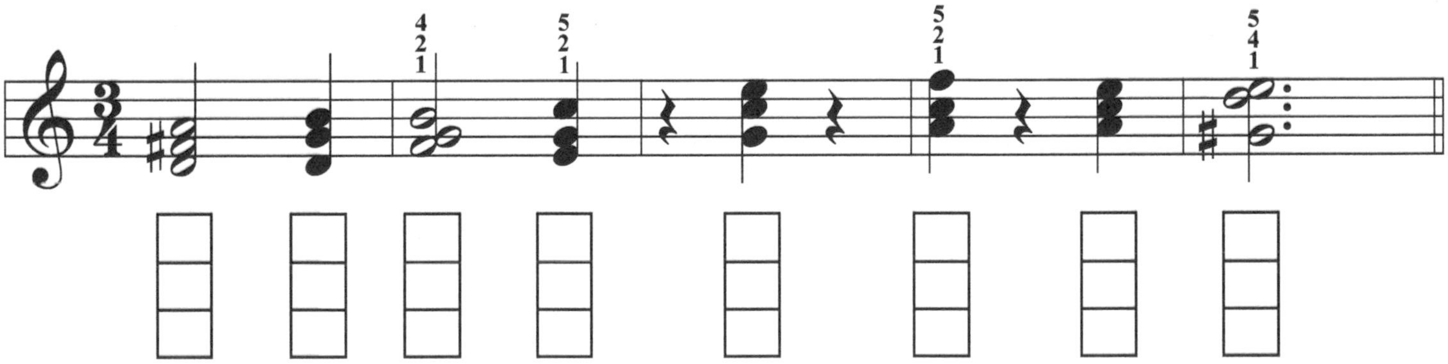

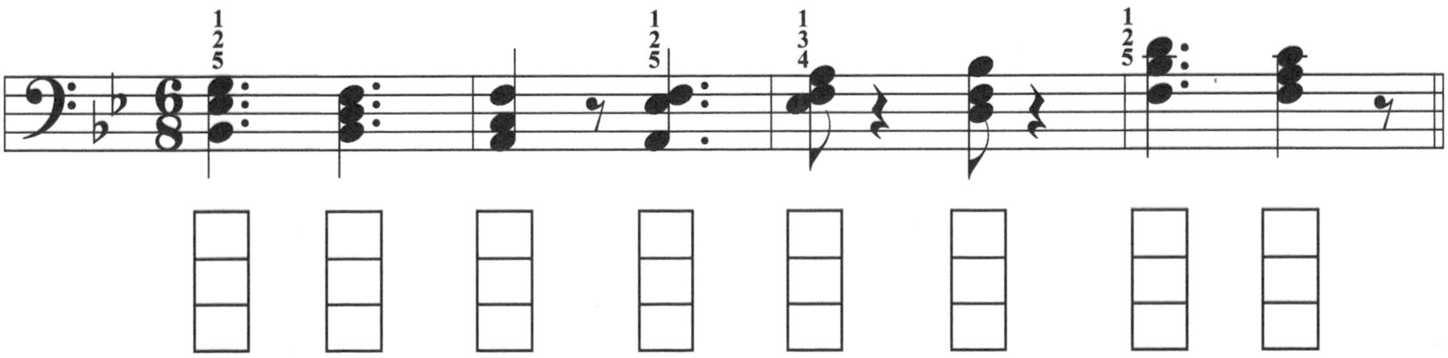

	A	A
	F	F
C	C	

KEYBOARD ASSIGNMENT: After completing the written work, play the chords in each measure. Do this at least three times per day. For extra work, add letter names in the blank boxes.

TEACHER'S NOTE: All chords on this page may be fingered using 1-3-5 (right hand) or 5-3-1 (left hand), *except* where other finger numbers are printed.

Lesson 17: Major Triads with Chord Symbols

Name____ Date________________ Score________________

A *major triad* is built using the 1st, 3rd and 5th degrees of any major scale. The chord name comes from the bottom note, called the *root*. The chord symbol is the same as the name of the root. Any chord may be used in different octaves of the keyboard and written in different clefs.

DIRECTIONS: Write the letter name of the *chord symbol* in the box above each chord. Look for *repeated notes* between chords.

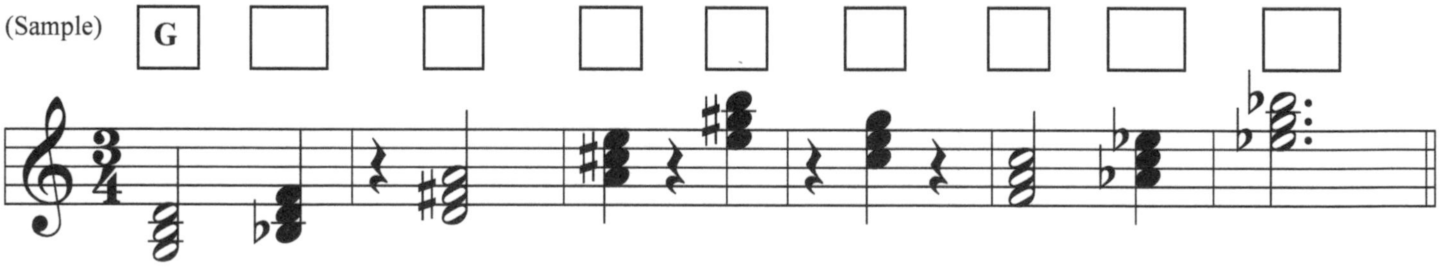

(Sample) G

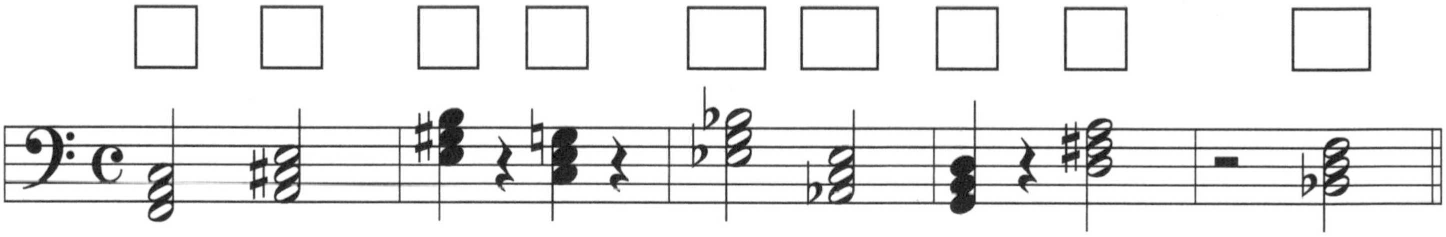

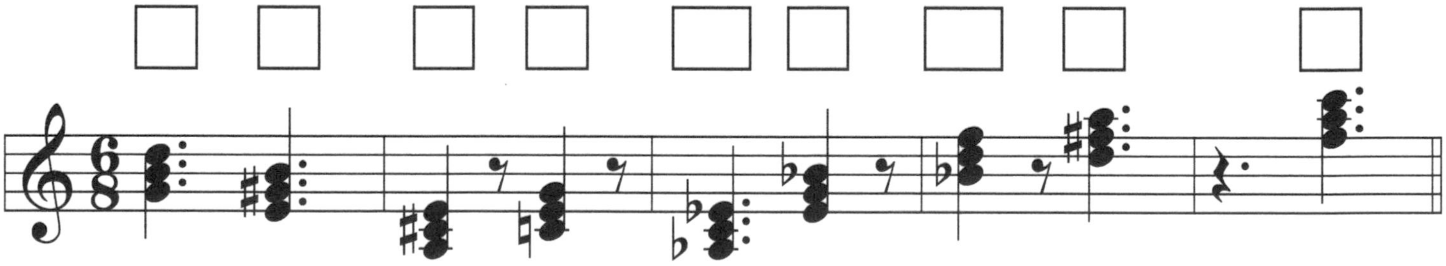

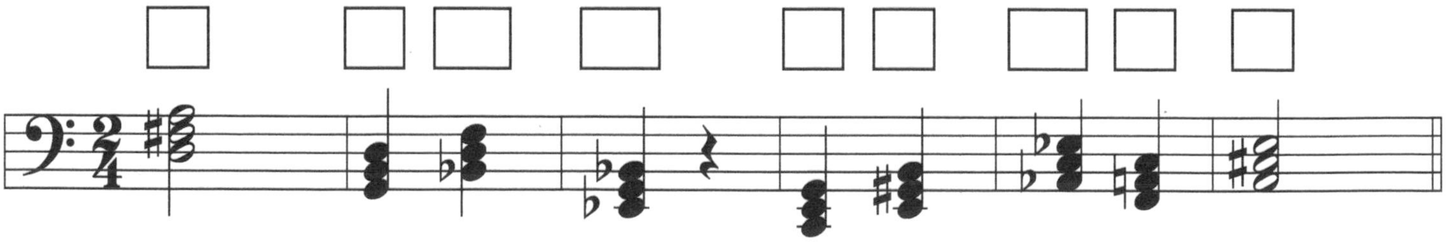

KEYBOARD ASSIGNMENT: Play the chords in each measure. Say the chord symbol name aloud as you play each chord. Do this at least three times per day. For extra practice, play each chord one octave higher or one octave lower than written.

Lesson 18: Chord Reading with Key Signatures

Name____Date__________________Score__________________

DIRECTIONS: Write the letter name of the *chord symbol* in the box above each chord. Look for *repeated notes* between chords.

KEYBOARD ASSIGNMENT: Play the chords in each measure. Say the chord symbol name aloud as you play each chord. Do this at least three times per day.

TEACHER'S NOTE: If desired, have the student add dotted lines to connect the *repeated notes*.

Lesson 19: Key Signature Reading with Accidentals

Name______________________________ Date________________ Score________________

DIRECTIONS: Write the letter name in the box under each note. Include a sharp, flat or natural as required by the key signature and accidentals. Remember that each accidental continues for the remainder of each measure until cancelled by the bar line.

KEYBOARD ASSIGNMENT: After completing the written work, play all notes at the keyboard at least three times per day. Say the letter names (with sharp, flat or natural) aloud as you play.

Lesson 20: Reading Small Changes of Intervals

Name ____________________ Date __________ Score __________

DIRECTIONS: Each measure contains one interval that is *different* from the others. Draw a circle around the *different* interval in each measure. Then write interval numbers in the boxes above each measure.

(Sample) 3rd 3rd 3rd 2nd

KEYBOARD ASSIGNMENT: After completing the written work, play the notes in each measure. Say the interval numbers aloud as you play. Do this at least three times per day.

Lesson 21: Changes in Clef

Name____ Date__________________ Score__________________

Treble and bass clefs can be used in *either* staff. The samples below show the normal clef positions and also clefs indicating *both hands* in treble staff and *both hands* in bass staff.

Changes of clef can happen *anywhere* in either staff, as circled in the sample lines below. The clefs in the middle of a measure are often *smaller* than the clefs at the beginning of the line.

DIRECTIONS: Draw a circle around all *clef changes* in each staff below.

KEYBOARD ASSIGNMENT: After completing the written work, play each line of music. Do this at least three times per day.

Lesson 22: Stem Placement on Intervals and Chords

Name____ Date____________________ Score____________________

Placement of a *stem* on the notes of an interval or chord is determined by the note which is the *biggest interval distance* from the *3rd staff line*.

In the line below, all stems go *down* on the *left* side of the notes.

In the line below, all stems go *up* on the *right* side of the notes.

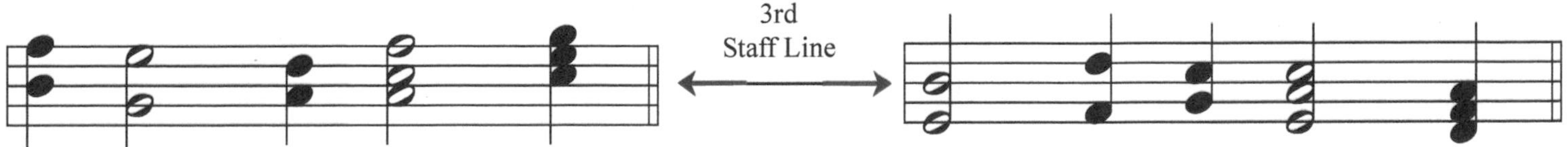

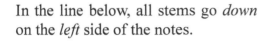

In the line below, the top and bottom notes are the *same interval distance* from the 3rd line. Therefore, the stems may *go either up or down.*

In intervals of a 2nd, the *lower* note is always on the *left*; the *upper* note is always on the *right*. The stem is placed in between.

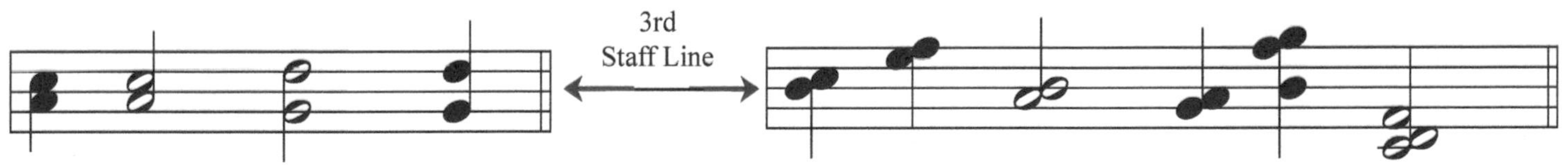

DIRECTIONS: Add stems to the following intervals and chords. Look at the samples above for help.

KEYBOARD ASSIGNMENT: After completing the written work, play all notes at the keyboard. Do this at least three times per day.

Lesson 23: Quick Interval Reading (2nds, 4ths and 6ths)

Name____Date__________________Score__________________

Intervals can be read much faster when your eye can recognize the distance between the two notes of the interval. ALWAYS READ the LOWEST NOTE FIRST.

EVEN numbered intervals (2nds, 4ths and 6ths) always have one note on a LINE and the other note in a SPACE. If the bottom note is on a *line*, the top note is in a *space* and vice-versa. The line below shows several different 2nds, 4ths and 6ths.

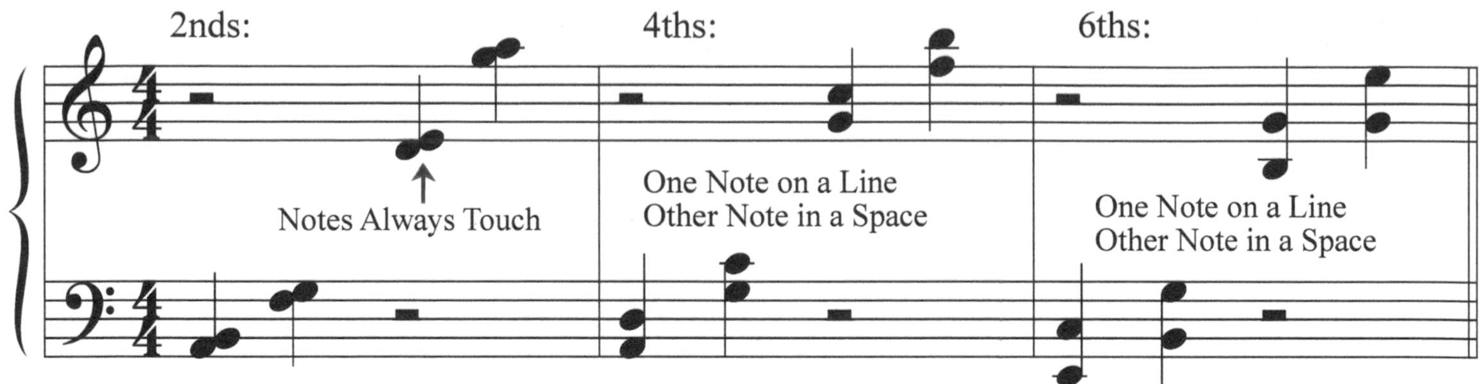

DIRECTIONS: Write the interval number in the box above each interval. Try NOT to think of the individual letter names of the notes. Instead, focus your eyes on the *distance* between the notes, using the guidelines above.

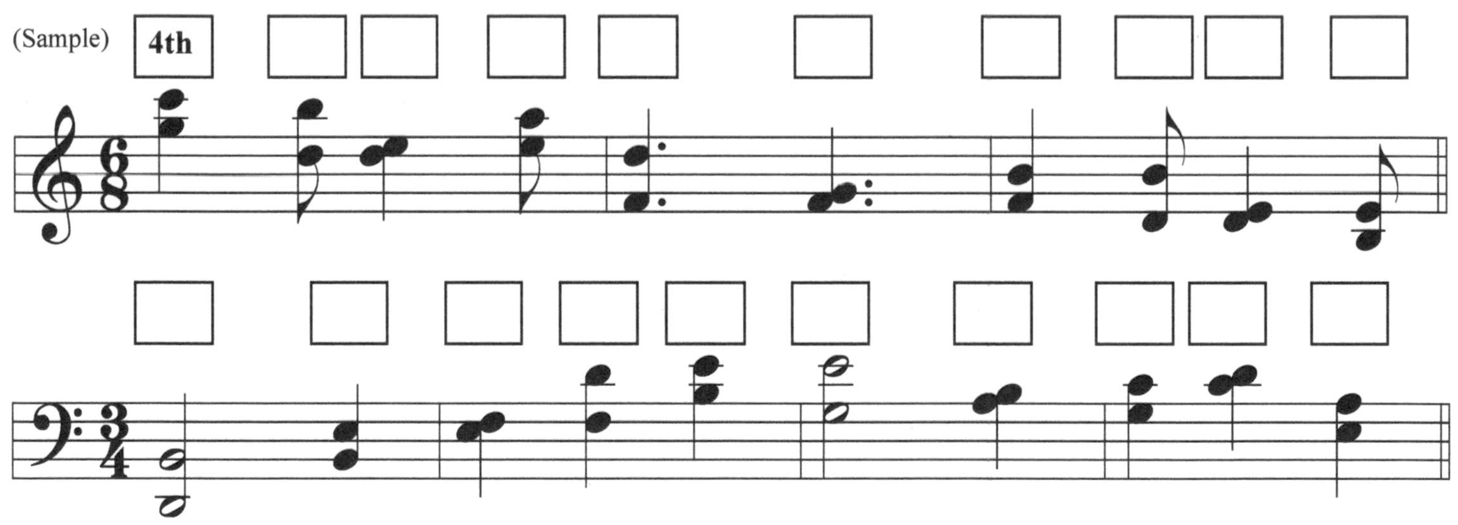

DIRECTIONS: Draw another quarter note *above* each printed note to make the interval indicated by the number. Add a stem to each interval.

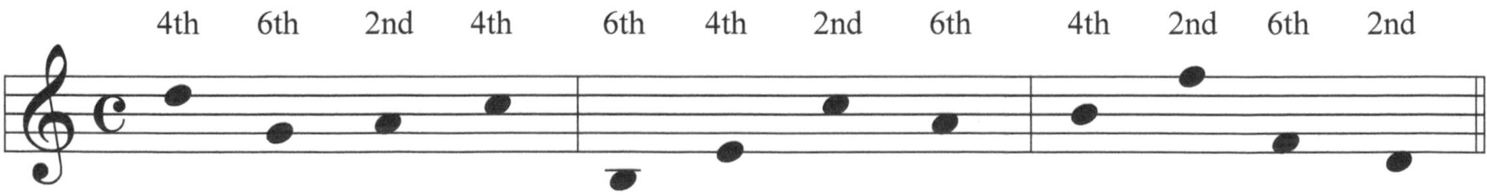

KEYBOARD ASSIGNMENT: After completing the written work, play all of the 2nds on this page. Next, play all of the 4ths. Then, play all of the 6ths.

For an extra assignment, play all of the intervals in the order as printed on this page; say the interval number aloud as you play.

Lesson 24: Quick Interval Reading (3rds, 5ths and 7ths)

Name______________________________ Date_______________ Score_______________

ODD numbered intervals (3rds, 5ths and 7ths) always have BOTH notes on a *line* or BOTH notes in a *space*. The line below shows several different 3rds, 5ths and 7ths.

DIRECTIONS: Write the interval number in the box above each interval. Try NOT to think of the individual letter names of the notes. Instead, focus your eyes on the *distance* between the notes, using the guidelines above.

DIRECTIONS: Draw another quarter note *above* the printed note to make the interval indicated by the number. Add a stem to each interval.

KEYBOARD ASSIGNMENT: After completing the written work, play all of the 3rds on this page. Next, play all of the 5ths. Then, play all of the 7ths.

For an extra assignment, play all of the intervals in the order as printed on this page; say the interval number aloud as you play.

Lesson 25: Natural Accents

Name ______________________ Date ______________ Score ______________

A *natural accent* is a small accent that is felt on the *first* count of every measure in *all* time signatures. Counts with natural accents are *circled* in the sample lines below. Natural accents are much less than the accent indicated by the mark: – . Natural accents are sometimes called *strong beats*; all other counts in a measure are normal beats (sometimes called *weak beats*).

In 4/4 and 6/8 time the middle count of each measure also has a natural accent (but *less* than the natural accent on the first count).

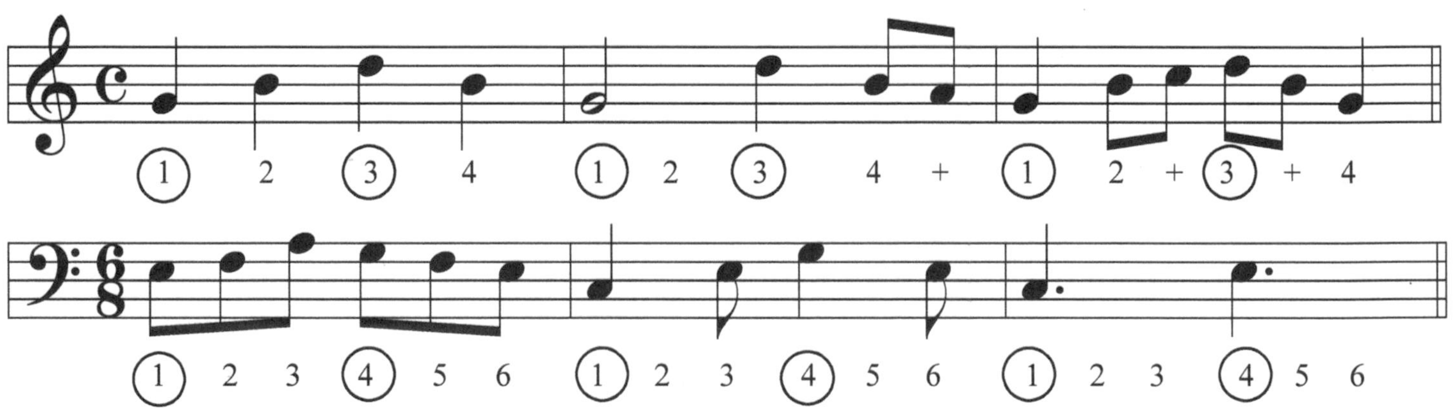

DIRECTIONS: Write the counting numbers on the dotted line below each measure. Then circle the numbers which are *natural accents.*

KEYBOARD ASSIGNMENT: After completing the written work, play all notes at the keyboard, giving a *small* accent to each count with a *natural accent*; count aloud as you play. Do this at least three times per day.

TEACHER'S NOTE: A natural accent is more an *implied* accent than a literal accent. In most music the natural accent is an internal pulse that helps the mind to organize the meter. Natural accents become prominent in music such as marches, waltzes and polkas where there is usually an emphasis on the first beat of each measure.

Lesson 26: Syncopated Rhythm

Name____Date______________________Score_____________________

Syncopation is a kind of rhythm that moves the accent away from the natural accent, from a strong beat to a normal beat. Longer notes on weak beats are one example of syncopation. The syncopated counts are circled in the two sample lines below. Tied notes are often a clue to syncopated rhythm.

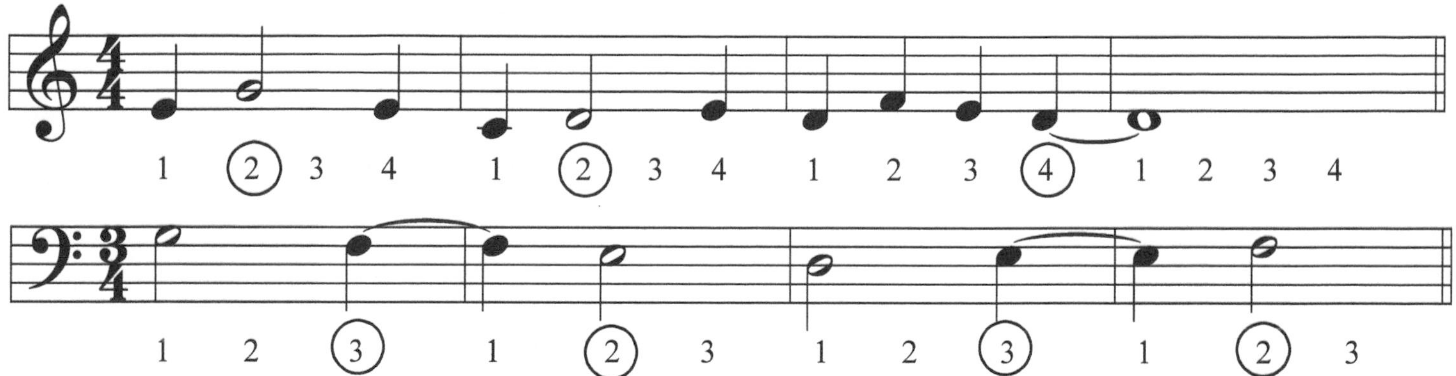

Another form of syncopation often occurs *between* the numbered beats of a measure. The syncopation is circled in the sample line below. Again, tied notes help to locate syncopated rhythm.

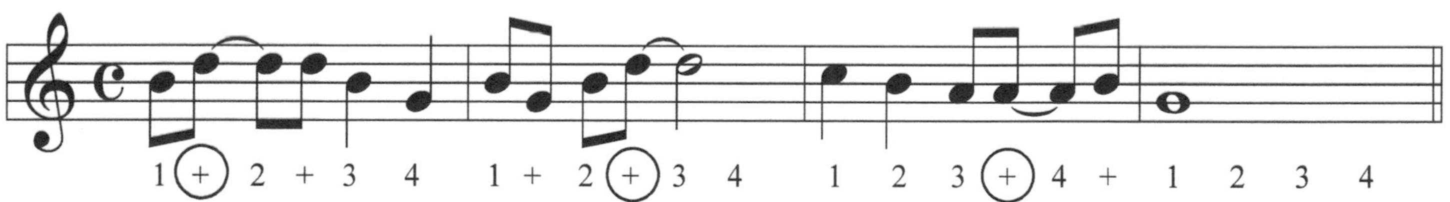

DIRECTIONS: Write the counting numbers on the dotted line below each measure. Then circle the places where syncopated accents occur.

KEYBOARD ASSIGNMENT: After completing the written work, play all notes at the keyboard, giving a *small* accent to each note that is *syncopated*; count aloud as you play. Do this at least three times per day.

TEACHER'S NOTE: The following books provide additional experience with syncopations: ***Schaum Easy Boogie, Book 1,*** and ***Schaum Rhythm & Blues, Book 1.***

Lesson 27: Transposing by Scale Degrees

Name____Date___________________Score___________________

To *transpose* a melody means to play it in a *different key*, starting on a higher or lower note. When transposing, you use a different *key signature*, notes from a different *scale* and a different *hand position.*

The first 7 notes of the scales of C, F and G Major are shown with their scale *degree numbers*. These will be used to help in transposing.

The first 4 measures of "America the Beautiful" are printed below in the key of *C Major*. Scale degree numbers have been written under each note.

DIRECTIONS: Write the scale degree numbers for "America the Beautiful" on the lines below each measure. Then write the *notes* for "America the Beautiful" in the key of *F Major*. The starting note is printed. Watch for different note values (half, quarter, eighth, etc.)

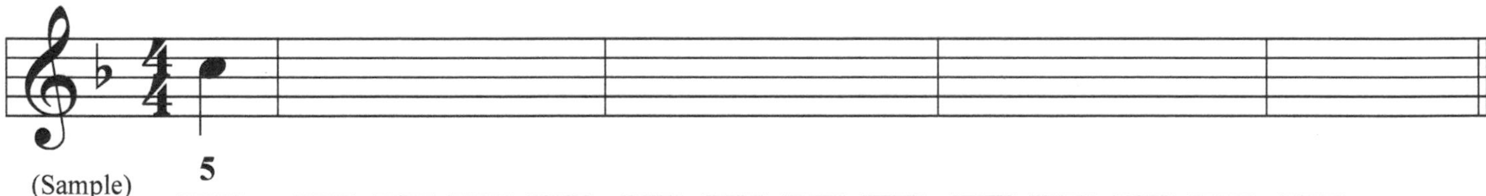

DIRECTIONS: Write the scale degree numbers for "America the Beautiful" on the lines below each measure. Then write the *notes* for "America the Beautiful" in the key of *G Major*. The starting note is printed.

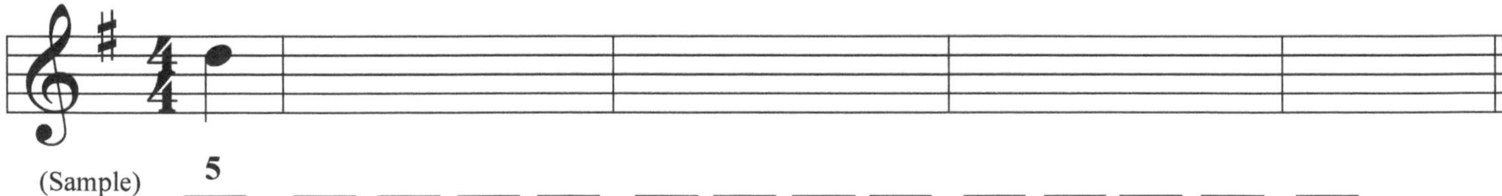

KEYBOARD ASSIGNMENT: After completing the written work, play "America the Beautiful" in all three keys. Do this at least three times per day. For an extra assignment, transpose "America the Beautiful" to the key of B-flat Major (see top of Lesson 28).

Lesson 28: More Transposing by Scale Degrees

Name_______________________________ Date_______________ Score_______________

The first 7 notes of the scales of D, B-flat and E-flat are shown with their scale *degree numbers*. These will be used to help in transposing.

Chord symbols can be transposed by scale degree the same as melody notes. The first 4 measures of "Lavender's Blue" are printed below in the key of *D Major* with chord symbols. This melody has a note which uses scale degree number 8 (one octave above the root).

DIRECTIONS: Write the scale *degree* numbers on the line below each note and also *above* each chord symbol.

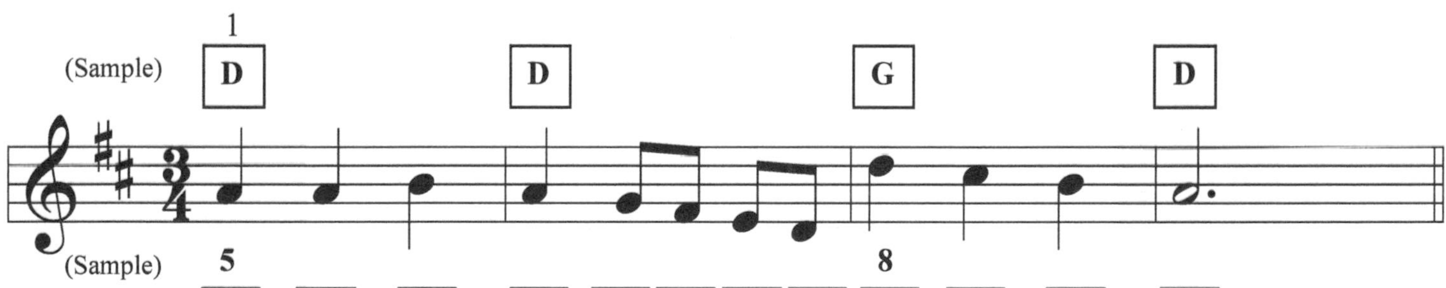

DIRECTIONS: Write the scale degree numbers for "Lavender's Blue" on the lines below each measure. Next, write the scale degree number for the *chord symbol* above each box. Then write the chord symbol *letter* in each box and the *notes* for "Lavender's Blue" in *B-flat Major*. The starting note is printed.

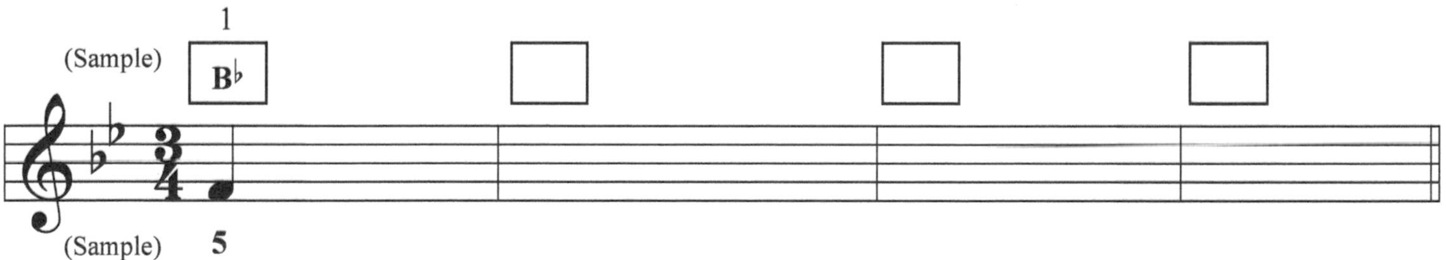

DIRECTIONS: Write the scale degree numbers for "Lavender's Blue" on the lines below each measure. Next, write the scale degree number for the *chord symbol* above each box. Then write the chord symbol *letter* in each box and the *notes* for "Lavender's Blue" in *E-flat Major*. The starting note is printed.

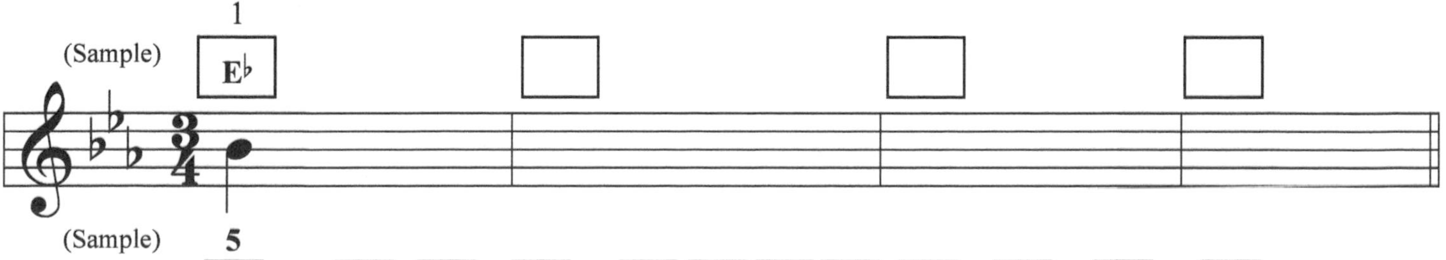

KEYBOARD ASSIGNMENT: After the written work is completed, play "Lavender's Blue" in all three keys using the chords as an accompaniment. Do this at least three times per day. For an extra assignment, transpose "Lavender's Blue" along with the chord symbols, to the key of *F Major*. (See top of Lesson 27.)

TEACHER'S NOTE: As an accompaniment, play one chord per measure on the first count. For some students, you may want to try other chord rhythms or broken chords. Schaum's ***Easy Keyboard Harmony, Book 1*** is recommended for further study in chords and accompaniments.

Lesson 29: 16th Notes and 3/8 Time Signature

Name____ Date_________________ Score_________________

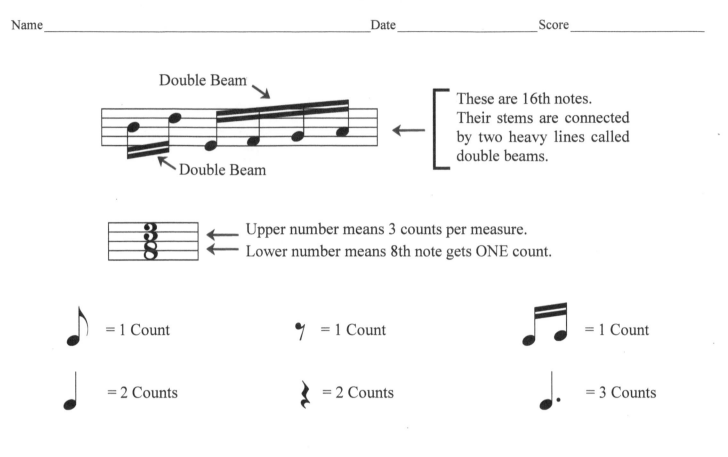

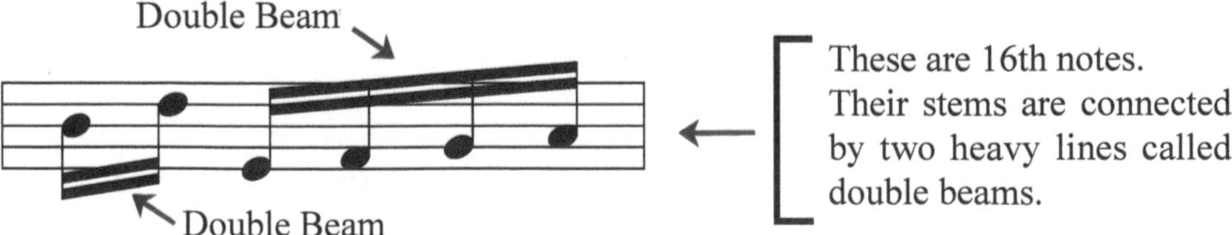

Upper number means 3 counts per measure.
Lower number means 8th note gets ONE count.

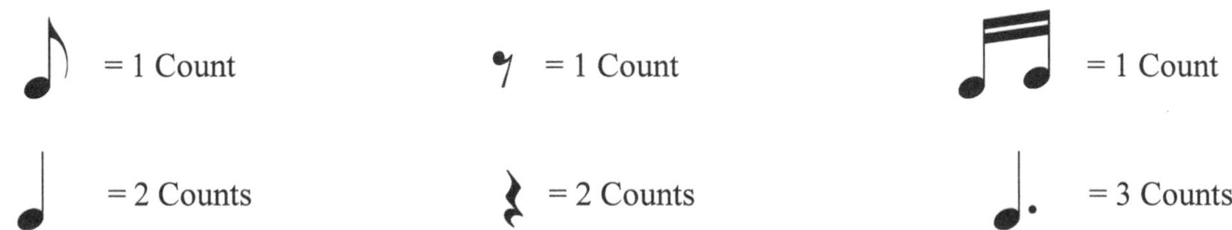

This line is a sample of counting in 3/8 time:

DIRECTIONS: Write the counting on the dotted lines below every measure.

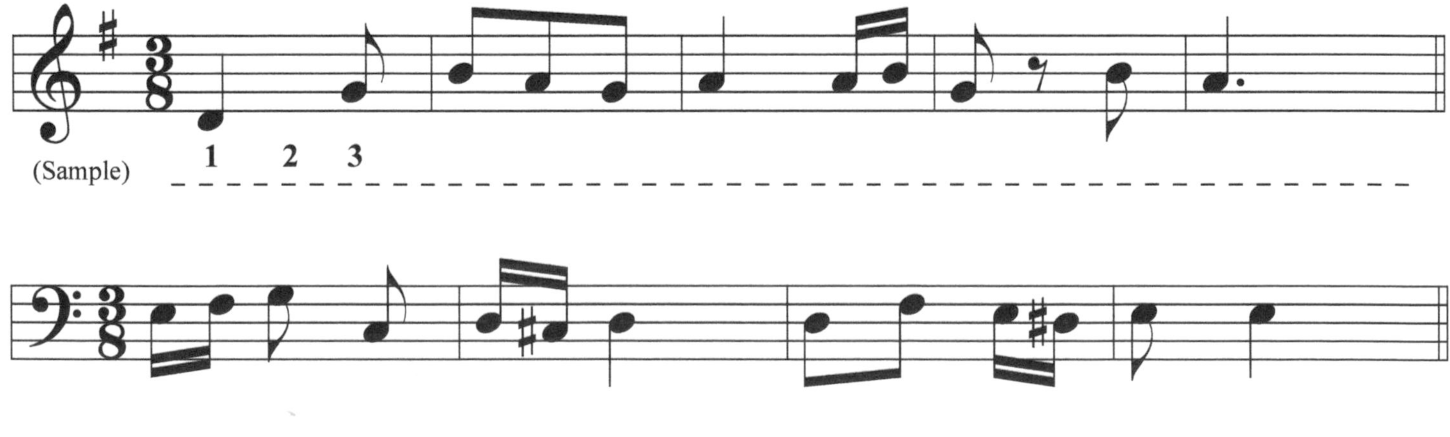

KEYBOARD ASSIGNMENT: After completing the written work, count aloud and clap hands, one clap for each note. Do this at least three times per day. For an extra assignment, the same measures may also be played at the keyboard while counting aloud.

TEACHER'S NOTE: It may be pointed out that note and rest values are the same in 6/8 time as in 3/8 time.

Lesson 30: 16th Notes in 4/4 Time

Name______________________________________Date__________________Score__________________

16th notes are often used in groups of four, as shown in the staff below. Notice that the counting is *different* in 4/4 time than in 3/8 time (as shown in Lesson 29).

DIRECTIONS: Write the counting on the dotted lines below every measure.

KEYBOARD ASSIGNMENT: After completing the written work, count aloud and play each line of music. Do this at least three times per day.

*TEACHER'S NOTE: You may prefer another way of subdividing the counts of the 16th notes. Four syllable words, such as "Mis-sis-sip-pi," and "Chat-ta-noo-ga" are possibilities.

Lesson 31: 16th Notes in 2/4 and 3/4 Time

Name____________________ Date____________ Score____________

16th notes often share a *beam* with 8th notes. Notice the counting written in the staffs below.

DIRECTIONS: Draw a circle around each pair of 16th notes in the staffs below. Write the counting on the dotted lines below every measure. Watch for changes of time signature.

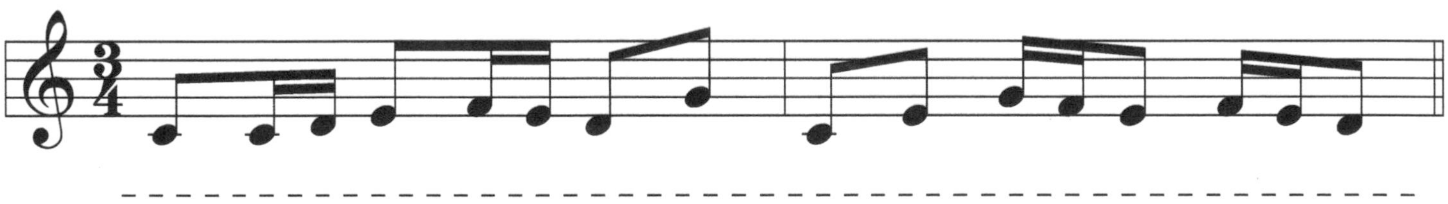

KEYBOARD ASSIGNMENT: After completing the written work, count aloud and play each line of music. Do this at least three times per day.